Attitude

Quote/Unquote

Applewood Books
Bedford, Massachusetts

Thank you for purchasing an Applewood Book. Applewood reprints America's lively classics—books from the past that are still of interest to modern reader For a free copy of our current catalog, please write to Applewood Books, P.O. Box 365, Bedford, MA 0173C

ISBN 1-55709-979-0

Library of Congress Control Number: 2001092161

10 9 8 7 6 5 4 3 2

Manufactured in U.S.A.

Introduction

It is amazing how often the over achievers in life are people with great attitudes. Attitudes that say "we can do it," "we can overcome" or that just see the silver lining in every dark cloud. People with great attitudes are fun to be around and enjoyable to work with.

The question we asked ourselves when creating this compilation is, "Why does it help to have a great attitude?" One reason (which can be found in the "Quote" side of this collection) is that a great attitude can be a positive force driving you toward success. Another reason (which can be found in the "Unquote" side of this collection) is that a great attitude can help you cope with the problems and overcome the obstacles that life puts in your path.

While we think that a great attitude helps you for both of the reasons mentioned above, we will leave it up to you to draw your own conclusions. Most of all, we hope that you enjoy this collection and find the wisdom and motivation to reinforce your great attitude and the great attitude of your team!

Quote

Nothing will work unless you do.

—John Wooden

Every calling is great when greatly pursued.

—Oliver Wendell Holmes

A healthy attitude is contagious but don't wait to catch it from others. Be a carrier.

—Source Unknown

Morale and attitude are the fundamental ingredients to success.

—Bud Wilkinson

If you doubt you can accomplish something, then you can't accomplish it. You have to have confidence in your ability, and then be tough enough to follow through.

—Rosalynn Carter

The future belongs to those who believe in the beauty of their dreams.

—Eleanor Roosevelt

Your attitude, not your aptitude, will determine your altitude.

—Zig Ziglar

To different minds, the same world is a hell, and a heaven.

—Ralph Waldo Emerson

Ability is what you're capable of doing. Motivation determines what you do. Attitude determines how well you do it.

—Lou Holtz

The ideal attitude is to be physically loose and mentally tight.

—Arthur Ashe

My father instilled in me the attitude of prevailing. If there's a challenge, go for it. If there's a wall to break down, break it down.

—Donny Osmond

I never had a policy; I have just tried to do my very best each and every day.

—Abraham Lincoln

I've learned from experience that the greater part of our happiness or misery depends on our dispositions and not on our circumstances.

—Martha Washington

Nothing can stop the man with the right mental attitude from achieving his goal; nothing on earth can help the man with the wrong mental attitude.

—Thomas Jefferson

It's faith in something and enthusiasm for something that makes a life worth living.

—Oliver Wendell Holmes

Life is not so much a matter of position as of disposition.

—Source Unknown

The starting point of all achievement is desire. Keep this constantly in mind. Weak desires bring weak results, just as a small amount of fire makes a small amount of heat.

—Napoleon Hill

To believe is to be strong. Doubt cramps energy. Belief is power.

—Frederick W. Robertson

You have to expect things of yourself before you can do them.

—Michael Jordan

Positive thinking will let you do everything better than negative thinking will.

—Zig Ziglar

This is the precept by which I have lived: Prepare for the worst; expect the best; and take what comes.

—Robert E. Speer

No pessimist ever discovered the secrets of the stars, or sailed to an uncharted land, or opened a new doorway for the human spirit.

—Helen Keller

Great effort springs naturally from a great attitude.

—Pat Riley

Never be afraid to try something new. Remember, amateurs built the ark. Professionals built the Titanic.

—Source Unknown

You can tell the size of a man by the size of the thing that makes him mad.

—Adlai E. Stevenson

Self-assurance is two-thirds of success.

—Proverb

Seek out that particular mental attribute which makes you feel most deeply and vitally alive, along with which comes the inner voice which says, "This is the real me," and when you have found that attitude, follow it.

—James Truslow Adams

The capacity for hope is the most significant fact of life. It provides human beings with a sense of destination and the energy to get started.

—Norman Cousins

We awaken in others the same attitude of mind we hold toward them.

—Elbert Hubbard

There is little difference in people, but that little difference makes a big difference. The little difference is attitude. The big difference is whether it is positive or negative.

—W. Clement Stone

A great attitude does much more than turn on the lights in our worlds; it seems to magically connect us to all sorts of serendipitous opportunities that were somehow absent before the change.

—Earl Nightingale

Only so far as a man believes strongly, mightily, can he act cheerfully, or do anything that is worth doing.

—Frederick W. Robertson

The difference between a successful person and others is not a lack of strength, not a lack of knowledge, but rather is a lack of will.

—Vince Lombardi

Your personal philosophy is the greatest determining factor in how your life works out.

—Jim Rohn

Consider the postage stamp: its usefulness consists in the ability to stick to one thing until it gets there.

—Josh Billings

Optimism is the faith that leads to achievement. Nothing can be done without hope and confidence.

—Helen Keller

Life is like a grindstone—whether it grinds you down or polishes you up depends on what you're made of.

—Source Unknown

Attitudes are the forerunners of conditions.

—Eric Butterworth

Pessimists choke in adversity. Optimists won't even let the rope grace their neck.

—Simon Cooper

We first must think "I can," then behave appropriately along that line of thought.

—Marsha Sinetar

"I can't do it" never yet accomplished anything; "I will try" has performed wonders.

—George Burnham

I've never run into a guy who could win at the top level in anything today and didn't have the right attitude, didn't give it everything he had, at least while he was doing it; wasn't prepared and didn't have the whole program worked out.

—Ted Turner

Let us show, not merely in great crises, but in every day affairs of life, qualities of practical intelligence, of hardiness and endurance, and above all, the power of devotion to a lofty ideal.

—Theodore Roosevelt

All our dreams can come true, if we have the courage to pursue them.

—Walt Disney

The miracle, or the power, that elevates the few is to be found in their industry, application, and perseverance under the prompting of a brave, determined spirit.

—Mark Twain

Persistent people begin their success where others end in failure.

—Edward Eggleston

The interest of being positive today will determine the incredible returns that await you tomorrow.

—Brian G. Jett

Good, better, best; never let it rest till your good is better and your better is best.

—Source Unknown

Minds are like parachutes—they work best when open.

—Sir James Dewar

The mind is the limit. As long as the mind can envision the fact that you can do something, you can do it—as long as you really believe 100%.

—Arnold Schwarzenegger

The greatest discovery of any generation is that a human being can alter his life by altering his attitude.

—William James

Everything in life is 95% attitude and 5% hope to gain. Translation: With the right attitude and a little bit of faith, you can move any mountain that comes in your way.

—Maria D. Pifferrer

When we think positively and imagine what we want, we risk disappointment; when we don't, we ensure it.

—Lana Limpert

Dwell in possibility.

—Emily Dickinson

Procrastination is the bad habit of putting off until the day after tomorrow what should have been done the day before yesterday.

—Napoleon Hill

Positive thinking is the key to success in business, education, pro football, anything that you can mention. I go out there thinking that I'm going to complete every pass.

—Ron Jaworski

It's not what you look at that matters, it's what you see...

—Henry David Thoreau

Leadership is practiced not so much in words as in attitude and in actions.

—Harold S. Geneen

Excellence is the result of caring more than others think is wise; risking more than others think is safe; dreaming more than others think is practical; and expecting more than others think is possible.

—Source Unknown

Opportunity lies in the man and not in the job.

—Zig Ziglar

Whether you think you can or think you can't, you're right.

—Henry Ford

I don't believe in pessimism. If something doesn't come up the way you want, forge ahead. If you think it's going to rain, it will.

—Clint Eastwood

It's not the size of the dog in the fight, but the size of the fight in the dog.

—Archie Griffin

We are all given a choice each day. We can react negatively to the demands made on us or we can choose to live abundantly, to transform the negative into the meaningful. Attitude is all. If I do not endow my life and my work with meaning, no one will ever be able to do it for me.

—Sarah Ban Breathnach

Our attitude toward life determines life's attitude towards us.

—Earl Nightingale

Nothing great was ever achieved without enthusiasm.

—Ralph Waldo Emerson

There is no chance, no destiny, no fate, that can circumvent or hinder or control the firm resolve of a determined soul.

—Ella Wheeler Wilcox

Yes, you can be a dreamer and a doer too, if you will remove one word from your vocabulary: impossible.

—Robert H. Schuller

Nothing splendid has ever been achieved except by those who dared believe that something inside them was superior to circumstance.

—Bruce Barton

You've got to take initiative and play your game—confidence makes the difference.

—Chris Evert

For every sale you miss because you're too enthusiastic, you will miss a hundred because you're not enthusiastic enough.

—Zig Ziglar

Believe and act as if it were impossible to fail.

—Charles F. Kettering

Unquote

One can never consent to creep when one feels an impulse to soar.

—Helen Keller

You can complain because roses have thorns, or you can rejoice because thorns have roses.

—Ziggy

If you don't like something, change it. If you can't change it, change your attitude.

—Maya Angelou

You cannot tailor make your situation in life, but you can tailor make your attitudes to fit those situations.

—Zig Ziglar

We must accept finite disappointment, but we must never lose infinite hope.

—Martin Luther King, Jr.

Courage and perseverance have a magical talisman, before which difficulties disappear and obstacles vanish into air.

—John Quincy Adams

It's not whether you get knocked down, it's whether you get up.

—Vince Lombardi

Energy and persistence conquer all things.

—Benjamin Franklin

I am only one, but still, I am one. I cannot do everything but I can do something. And, because I cannot do everything, I will not refuse to do what I can.

—Edward Everett Hale

When you face your fear, most of the time you will discover that it was not really such a big threat after all. We all need some form of deeply rooted, powerful motivation—it empowers us to overcome obstacles so we can live our dreams.

—Les Brown

Being challenged in life is inevitable, being defeated is optional.

—Roger Crawford

Adversity causes some men to break; others to break records.

—William A. Ward

We must build dikes of courage to hold back the flood of fear.

—Martin Luther King, Jr.

It's a little like wrestling a gorilla. You don't quit when you're tired, you quit when the gorilla is tired.

—Robert Strauss

When you get into a tight place and everything goes against you, till it seems as though you could not hold on a minute longer, never give up then, for that is just the place and time that the tide will turn.

—Harriet Beecher Stowe

I never failed once. It just happened to be a 2000-step process.

—Thomas A. Edison

The marvelous richness of human experience would lose something of rewarding joy if there were no limitations to overcome. The hilltop hour would not be half so wonderful if there were no dark valleys to traverse.

—Helen Keller

What happens is not as important as how you react to what happens.

—Thaddeus Golas

The remarkable thing is, we have a choice everyday regarding the attitude we will embrace for that day.

—Charles Swindoll

Failure is a detour, not a dead-end street.

—Zig Ziglar

Keep on beginning and failing. Each time you fail, start all over again, and you will grow stronger until you have accomplished a purpose—not the one you began with perhaps, but one you'll be glad to remember.

—Anne Sullivan

Every tomorrow has two handles. We can take hold of it with the handle of anxiety or the handle of faith.

—Henry Ward Beecher

Finish each day and be done with it. You have done what you could. Some blunders and absurdities no doubt crept in; forget them as soon as you can. Tomorrow is a new day; begin it well and serenely and with too high a spirit to be encumbered with your old nonsense.

—Ralph Waldo Emerson

No man is ever whipped until he quits in his own mind.

—Napoleon Hill

God grant me the serenity to accept the things I cannot change, the courage to change the things I can, and the wisdom to know the difference.

—Reinhold Niebuhr

We cannot change our past. We cannot change the fact that people act in a certain way. We cannot change the inevitable. The only thing we can do is play on the one string we have, and that is our attitude.

—Charles Swindoll

Nothing in life is so hard that you can't make it easier by the way you take it.

—Ellen Glasgow

My attitude is that if you push me towards something that you think is a weakness, then I will turn that perceived weakness into a strength.

—Michael Jordan

Failure is the opportunity to begin again, more intelligently.

—Henry Ford

A little more persistence, a little more effort, and what seemed hopeless failure may turn to glorious success.

—Elbert Hubbard

Far better is it to dare mighty things, to win glorious triumphs, even though checkered by failure, than to rank with those poor spirits who neither enjoy nor suffer much, because they live in the gray twilight that knows not victory nor defeat.

—Theodore Roosevelt

It's hard to beat a person who never gives up.

—Babe Ruth

The only disability in life is a bad attitude.

—Scott Hamilton

T'is easy enough to be pleasant,
When life flows along like a song;
But the man worth while is the one who will smile
When everything goes dead wrong.

—Ella Wheeler Wilcox

Walk through the valleys with optimism of the mountaintops ahead.

—Simon Cooper

Most people fail in life because they major in minor things.

—Tony Robbins

The minute you start talking about what you're going to do if you lose, you have lost.

—George Shultz

If you've learned from losing, it wasn't a loss.

—Brian G. Jett

I have discovered that those who constantly complain will in their very circumstances constantly remain.

—Brian G. Jett

My motto was always to keep swinging. Whether I was in a slump or feeling badly or having trouble off the field, the only thing to do was keep swinging.

—Hank Aaron

A pound of pluck is worth a ton of luck.

—James A. Garfield

It's not who you are that holds you back, it's who you think you're not.

—Source Unknown

When I have fully decided that a result is worth getting, I go ahead of it and make trial after trial until it comes.

—Thomas A. Edison

The only difference between a good day and a bad day is your ATTITUDE!

—Dennis S. Brown

Never give up. Keep your thoughts and your mind always on the goal.

—Tom Bradley

A failure is not always a mistake, it may simply be the best one can do under the circumstances. The real mistake is to stop trying.

—B. F. Skinner

Lots of people limit their possibilities by giving up easily. Never tell yourself this is too much for me. It's no use. I can't go on. If you do you're licked, and by your own thinking, too. Keep believing and keep on keeping on.

—Norman Vincent Peale

A strong positive attitude will create more miracles than any wonder drug.

—Patricia Neal

Some men have thousands of reasons why they cannot do what they want to; all they need is one reason why they can.

—Willis Whitney

The difference between perseverance and obstinacy is that one comes from a strong will, and the other from a strong won't.

—Henry Ward Beecher

The manner in which one endures what must be endured is more important than the thing that must be endured.

—Dean Acheson

The difference between the impossible and the possible lies in a person's determination.

—Tommy Lasorda

Be of good cheer. Do not think of today's failures, but of the success that may come tomorrow. You have set yourselves a difficult task, but you will succeed if you persevere; and you will find joy in overcoming obstacles. Remember, no effort that we make to attain something beautiful is ever lost.

—Helen Keller

When life hands you lemons, make lemonade!

—Source Unknown

There are two big forces at work, external and internal. We have very little control over external forces such as tornadoes, earthquakes, floods, disasters, illness and pain. What really matters is the internal force. How do I respond to those disasters?

—Leo F. Buscaglia

Problems are only opportunities in work clothes.

—Henry J. Kaiser

Victory is always possible for the person who refuses to stop fighting.

—Napoleon Hill

It's not the load that breaks you down, it's the way you carry it.

—Lena Horne

Difficulties are meant to rouse, not discourage. The human spirit is to grow strong by conflict.

—William Ellery Channing

Obstacles don't have to stop you. If you run into a wall, don't turn around and give up. Figure out how to climb it, go through it, or work around it.

—Michael Jordan

A will finds a way.

—Orison Swett Marden

You cannot control what happens to you, but you can control your attitude toward what happens to you, and in that, you will be mastering change rather than allowing it to master you.

—Brian Tracy

What happens to a man is less significant than what happens within him.

—Louis L. Mann

The greatest test of courage on earth is to bear defeat without losing heart.

—Robert Green Ingersoll

Life is too serious to be taken seriously.

—Mike Leonard

I have discovered that patience is not the ability to wait, but the ability to keep a good attitude while waiting.

—Joyce Meyer

Remember no one can make you feel inferior without your consent.

—Eleanor Roosevelt

Self-pity is our worst enemy and if we yield to it, we can never do anything wise in this world.

—Helen Keller

Life can be wildly tragic at times, and I've had my share. But whatever happens to you, you have to keep a slightly comic attitude. In the final analysis, you have got not to forget to laugh.

—Katharine Hepburn

Your living is determined not so much by what life brings to you as by the attitude you bring to life; not so much by what happens to you as by the way your mind looks at what happens.

—John Homer Miller

You are never a loser until you quit trying.

—Mike Ditka

Being defeated is often a temporary condition. Giving up is what makes it permanent.

—Marilyn vos Savant

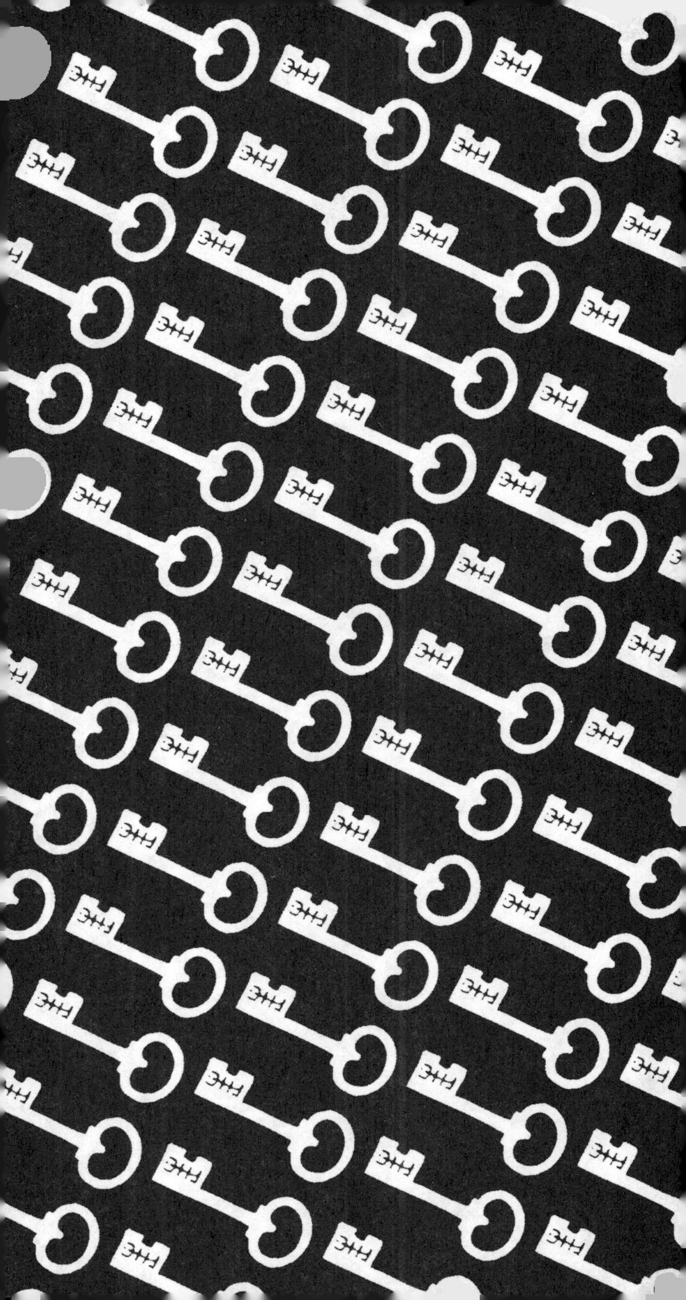

Success

Quote/Unquote

Applewood Books
Bedford, Massachusetts

Thank you for purchasing an Applewood Book. Applewood reprints America's lively classics—books from the past that are still of interest to modern reader For a free copy of our current catalog, please write to Applewood Books, P.O. Box 365, Bedford, MA 01730

ISBN 1-55709-975-8

Library of Congress Control Number: 2001092157

10 9 8 7 6 5 4 3 2

Manufactured in U.S.A.

Introduction

Success . . . it is the holy grail that we all seek. Whether it is on the job, on the field, in the community, at home or just at life in general . . . we all want to be successful.

When creating this compilation we asked ourselves two questions. The first is, "What is success (and what isn't success)?" and the second is, "What does it take to succeed?" We endeavor to answer the first question in the "Quote" side of this collection by sharing quotations about the meaning of success. In the "Unquote" side of this collection, we endeavor to answer the second question by providing tips from experts throughout the ages on how to achieve success.

We think that individuals and organizations alike will benefit from this collection and we encourage you to share the insights that you find in this book. Most of all, we hope that you enjoy this collection and find the wisdom and motivation to achieve success in your life!

Quote

Success is following the pattern of life one enjoys most.

—Al Capp

Success is sweet and sweeter if long delayed and gotten through many struggles and defeats.

—Amos Bronson Alcott

In America, everything you need to succeed is within reach.

—Jim Rohn

It is hard to fail, but it is worse never to have tried to succeed. In this life we get nothing save by effort.

—Theodore Roosevelt

Winning is not a sometime thing, it's an all time thing. You don't win once in a while, you don't do things right once in a while, you do them right all the time. Winning is habit. Unfortunately, so is losing.

—Vince Lombardi

The reward of a thing well done is to have done it.

—Ralph Waldo Emerson

You always pass failure on the way to success.

—Mickey Rooney

Most people who succeed in the face of seemingly impossible conditions are people who simply don't know how to quit.

—Robert H. Schuller

Success, or failure, very often arrives on wings that seem mysterious to us.

—Dr. Marcus Bach

There is no point at which you can say, "Well, I'm successful now. I might as well take a nap."

—Carrie Fisher

Success isn't how far you got, but the distance you traveled from where you started.

—Source Unknown

Failure is a detour, not a dead-end street.

—Zig Ziglar

Success is to be measured not so much by the position that one has reached in life as by the obstacles which one has overcome while trying to succeed.

—Booker T. Washington

Success is not a harbor but a voyage with its own perils to the spirit. The game of life is to come up a winner, to be a success, or to achieve what we set out to do.

—Richard M. Nixon

I honestly think it is better to be a failure at something you love than to be a success at something you hate.

—George Burns

The talent of success is nothing more than doing what you can do well, and doing well whatever you do.

—Henry Wadsworth Longfellow

Ninety-nine percent of the failures come from people who have the habit of making excuses.

—George Washington Carver

When you get into a tight place and everything goes against you, till it seems as though you could not hold on a minute longer, never give up then, for that is just the place and time that the tide will turn.

—Harriet Beecher Stowe

All human beings have failings, all human beings have needs and temptations and stresses. Men and women who live together through long years get to know one another's failings; but they also come to know what is worthy of respect and admiration in those they live with and in themselves. If at the end one can say, This man used to the limit the powers that God granted him; he was worthy of love and respect and of the sacrifices of many people, made in order that he might achieve what he deemed to be his task, then that life has been lived well and there are no regrets.

—Eleanor Roosevelt

People fail forward to success.

—Mary Kay Ash

Success is a journey, not a destination.

—Ben Sweetland

You are not here to fritter away your precious hours when you have the ability to accomplish so much by making a slight change in your routine. No more hiding from success. Leave time, leave space, to grow. Now.

—Og Mandino

Before success in any man's life he is sure to meet with much temporary defeat and, perhaps, some failure. When defeat overtakes a man, the easiest and most logical thing to do is to quit. That is exactly what the majority of men do.

—Napoleon Hill

We want to be first; not first if, not first but; but first!

—John F. Kennedy

There is no happiness except in the realization that we have accomplished something.

—Henry Ford

I don't know the key to success, but the key to failure is trying to please everybody.

—Bill Cosby

Never continue in a job you don't enjoy. If you're happy in what you're doing, you'll like yourself, you'll have inner peace. And if you have that, along with physical health, you will have had more success than you could possibly have imagined.

—Johnny Carson

The man who makes no mistakes does not usually make anything.

—Theodore Roosevelt

Keep in mind that neither success nor failure is ever final.

—Roger Babson

One's best success comes after their greatest disappointments.

—Henry Ward Beecher

Many of life's failures are people who did not realize how close they were to success when they gave up.

—Thomas A. Edison

Success is but a loose stone on the vast rocks of failure.

—Source Unknown

Success is a progressive realization of worthwhile, predetermined personal goals.

—Paul J. Meyer

There is little success where there is little laughter.

—Andrew Carnegie

The twin killers of success are impatience and greed.

—Jim Rohn

Not many people are willing to give failure a second opportunity. They fail once and it is all over. The bitter pill of failure is often more than most people can handle. If you are willing to accept failure and learn from it, if you are willing to consider failure as a blessing in disguise and bounce back, you have got the essential of harnessing one of the most powerful success forces.

—Joseph Sugarman

There are two kinds of success. One is the very rare kind that comes to the man who has the power to do what no one else has the power to do. That is genius. But the average man who wins what we call success is not a genius. He is a man who has merely the ordinary qualities that he shares with his fellows, but who has developed those ordinary qualities to a more than ordinary degree.

—Theodore Roosevelt

Victory is sweetest when you've known defeat.

—Malcolm S. Forbes

If you have made mistakes, even serious ones, there is always another chance for you. What we call failure is not the falling down, but the staying down.

—Mary Pickford

The road to success is always under construction.

—Lily Tomlin

Success is not to know the most about what you do, it is to do the most about what you don't know.

—Source Unknown

Men succeed when they realize that their failures are the preparation for their victories.

—Ralph Waldo Emerson

My great concern is not whether you have failed, but whether you are content with your failure.

—Abraham Lincoln

You may be disappointed if you fail, but you are doomed if you don't try.

—Beverly Sills

The only honest measure of your success is what you are doing compared to your true potential.

—Paul J. Meyer

How many a man has thrown up his hands at a time when a little more effort, a little more patience would have achieved success.

—Elbert Hubbard

The minute you start talking about what you're going to do if you lose, you have lost.

—George Shultz

Success in its highest and noblest form calls for peace of mind and enjoyment and happiness which come only to the man who has found the work that he likes best.

—Napoleon Hill

When nothing seems to help, I'd look at one of my stonecutters hammering away at a rock, perhaps a hundred times without as much as a crack showing in it. Yet, at the hundred and first blow it would split in two, and I knew it was not that blow that did it, but all that had gone before.

—Jacob Riis

When all is said and done, success without happiness is the worst kind of failure.

—Louis Binstock

Each success only buys an admission ticket to a more difficult problem.

—Henry Kissinger

When you get right down to the root meaning of the word "succeed" you find that it simply means to follow through.

—F. W. Nichol

Coming together is a beginning, staying together is progress and working together is success.

—Henry Ford

A man is a success if he gets up in the morning and gets to bed at night and in between he does what he wants to do.

—Bob Dylan

It's not whether you get knocked down, it's whether you get up.

—Vince Lombardi

The only failure a man ought to fear is failure in cleaving to the purpose he sees to be best.

—T. S. Eliot

Success without honor is an unseasoned dish; it will satisfy your hunger, but it won't taste good.

—Joe Paterno

People who do not succeed have one distinguishing trait in common. They know all the reasons for failure and have what they believe to be air-tight alibis to explain their own lack of achievement.

—Napoleon Hill

Success is the prize for those who stand true to their ideas.

—Josh Hinds

Success doesn't mean the absence of failures; it means the attainment of ultimate objectives. It means winning the war, not every battle.

—Edwin C. Bliss

Procrastination is the fear of success. People procrastinate because they are afraid of the success that they know will result if they move ahead now. Because success is heavy, carries a responsibility with it, it is much easier to procrastinate and live on the "someday I'll" philosophy.

—Denis Waitley

However things may seem, no evil thing is success and no good thing is failure.

—Henry Wadsworth Longfellow

No one can possibly achieve any real and lasting success or "get rich" in business by being a conformist.

—J. Paul Getty

Most people give up just when they're about to achieve success. They quit on the one yard line. They give up at the last minute of the game, one foot from a winning touchdown.

—H. Ross Perot

Where I was born and where and how I have lived is unimportant. It is what I have done with where I have been that should be of interest.

—Georgia O'Keeffe

That some achieve great success, is proof to all that others can achieve it as well.

—Abraham Lincoln

A failure is a man who has blundered, but is not able to cash in on the experience.

—Elbert Hubbard

Being defeated is often a temporary condition. Giving up is what makes it permanent.

—Marilyn vos Savant

I firmly believe that any man's finest hour, the greatest fulfillment of all that he holds dear, is that moment when he has worked his heart out in a good cause and lies exhausted on the field of battle—victorious.

—Vince Lombardi

Success is relevant to coping with obstacles . . . but no problem is ever solved by those, who, when they fail, look for someone to blame instead of something to do.

—Fred Waggoner

Success is always temporary. When all is said and done, the only thing you'll have left is your character.

—Vince Gill

Show me a thoroughly satisfied man and I will show you a failure.

—Thomas A. Edison

THE Unquote

Everything comes to him who hustles while he waits.

—Henry Ford

I found that the men and women who got to the top were those who did the jobs they had in hand, with everything they had of energy and enthusiasm and hard work.

—Harry S Truman

The real secret of success is enthusiasm.

—Walter Chrysler

Sweat plus sacrifice equals success.

—Charlie Finley

The most successful men in the end are those whose success is the result of steady accretion. It is the man who carefully advances step by step, with his mind becoming wider and wider—and progressively better able to grasp any theme or situation—persevering in what he knows to be practical, and concentrating his thought upon it, who is bound to succeed in the greatest degree.

—Alexander Graham Bell

The dictionary is the only place that success comes before work.

—Arthur Brisbane

If you want to increase your success rate, double your failure rate.

—Tom Watson

It had long since come to my attention that people of accomplishment rarely sat back and let things happen to them. They went out and happened to things.

—Elinor Smith

Success is a state of mind. If you want success, start thinking of yourself as a success.

—Dr. Joyce Brothers

Go forward confidently, energetically attacking problems, expecting favorable outcomes.

—Norman Vincent Peale

Success is the result of perfection, hard work, learning from failure, loyalty, and persistence.

—Colin Powell

Don't bother just to be better than your contemporaries or predecessors. Try to be better than yourself.

—William Faulkner

Do it now. You become successful the moment you start moving toward a worthwhile goal.

—Samuel Insull

Some people dream of success...while others wake up and work hard at it.

—Source Unknown

Edison failed 10,000 times before he made the electric light. Do not be discouraged if you fail a few times.

—Napoleon Hill

Eighty percent of success is showing up.

—Woody Allen

Success comes from taking the initiative and following up . . . persisting . . . eloquently expressing the depth of your love. What simple action could you take today to produce a new momentum toward success in your life?

—Tony Robbins

Success seems to be largely a matter of hanging on after others have let go.

—William Feather

There is no chance, no destiny, no fate, that can circumvent or hinder or control the firm resolve of a determined soul.

—Ella Wheeler Wilcox

There little more persistence, a little more effort, and what seemed hopeless failure may turn to glorious success.

—Elbert Hubbard

Success seems to be connected with action. Successful men keep moving. They make mistakes, but they don't quit.

—Conrad Hilton

We must walk consciously only part way toward our goal, and then leap in the dark to our success.

—Henry David Thoreau

I am not judged by the number of times I fail, but by the number of times I succeed: and the number of times I succeed is in direct proportion to the number of times I fail and keep trying.

—Tom Hopkins

Nothing splendid has ever been achieved except by those who dared believe that something inside them was superior to circumstance.

—Bruce Barton

Only those who dare to fail greatly can ever achieve greatly.

—Robert F. Kennedy

Success in business requires training and discipline and hard work. But if you're not frightened by these things, the opportunities are just as great today as they ever were.

—David Rockefeller

The person interested in success has to learn to view failure as a healthy, inevitable part of the process of getting to the top.

—Dr. Joyce Brothers

Success usually comes to those who are too busy to be looking for it.

—Henry David Thoreau

Press on: nothing in the world can take the place of perseverance. Talent will not; nothing is more common than unsuccessful men with talent. Genius will not; unrewarded genius is almost a proverb. Education will not; the world is full of educated derelicts. Persistence and determination alone are omnipotent.

—Calvin Coolidge

If A equals success, then the formula is: A=X+Y+Z. X is work. Y is play. Z is keep your mouth shut.

—Albert Einstein

If you want to succeed you should strike out on new paths rather than travel the worn paths of accepted success.

—John D. Rockefeller, Jr.

For you to be successful, sacrifices must be made. It's better that they are made by others but failing that, you'll have to make them yourself.

—Rita Mae Brown

Nothing can stop the man with the right mental attitude from achieving his goal; nothing on earth can help the man with the wrong mental attitude.

—Thomas Jefferson

To be successful, the first thing to do is fall in love with your work.

—Sister Mary Lauretta

One essential to success is that your desire be an all-obsessing one, your thoughts and aims be co-ordinated, and your energy be concentrated and applied without letup.

—Claude M. Bristol

People with goals succeed because they know where they're going.

—Earl Nightingale

No one gets an iron-clad guarantee of success. Certainly, factors like opportunity, luck and timing are important. But the backbone of success is usually found in old fashioned, basic concepts like hard work, determination, good planning and perseverance.

—Merlin Olsen

Success is often the result of taking a misstep in the right direction.

—Al Bernstein

Aim for the highest.

—Andrew Carnegie

Victory is always possible for the person who refuses to stop fighting.

—Napoleon Hill

A competitor will find a way to win. Competitors take bad breaks and use them to drive themselves just that much harder. Quitters take bad breaks and use them as reasons to give up. It's all a matter of pride.

—Nancy Lopez

The most important single ingredient in the formula of success is knowing how to get along with people.

—Theodore Roosevelt

I hated every minute of training, but I said, "Don't quit. Suffer now and live the rest of your life as a champion."

—Muhammad Ali

Commit yourself to a dream. Nobody who tries to do something great but fails is a total failure. Why? Because he can always rest assured that he succeeded in life's most important battle—he defeated the fear of trying.

—Robert H. Schuller

To succeed in business it is necessary to make others see things as you see them.

—John H. Patterson

Hold yourself responsible to a higher standard than anybody else expects of you; never excuse yourself.

—Henry Ward Beecher

Most of the successful people I've known are the ones who do more listening than talking.

—Bernard M. Baruch

You can have anything you want—if you want it badly enough. You can be anything you want to be, do anything you set out to accomplish if you hold to that desire with singleness of purpose.

—Abraham Lincoln

The victory of success is half done when one gains the habit of work.

—Sarah Knowles Bolton

Success follows doing what you want to do. There is no other way to be successful.

—Malcolm S. Forbes

A man can succeed at almost anything for which he has unlimited enthusiasm.

—Charles M. Schwab

Forget mistakes. Forget failure. Forget everything except what you're going to do now, and do it.

—Will Durant

I do not think that there is any other quality so essential to success of any kind as the quality of perseverance. It overcomes almost everything, even nature.

—John D. Rockefeller

Persistent people begin their success where others end in failure.

—Edward Eggleston

Do not be discouraged if your plans do not succeed the first time. No one learns to walk by taking only one step.

—Catherine Pulsifer

Of course there is no formula for success except perhaps an unconditional acceptance of life and what it brings.

—Artur Rubinstein

Average people look for ways of getting away with it; successful people look for ways of getting on with it.

—Jim Rohn

Ability may get you to the top, but it takes character to keep you there.

—John Wooden

To keep our faces toward change, and behave like free spirits in the presence of fate, is strength undefeatable.

—Helen Keller

Success is not the result of spontaneous combustion. You must set yourself on fire.

—Source Unknown

One important key to success is self-confidence. An important key to self-confidence is preparation.

—Arthur Ashe

Plan to succeed, or you have planned to fail.

—Donald Hall

The difference between a successful person and others is not a lack of strength, not a lack of knowledge, but rather is a lack of will.

—Vince Lombardi

Flaming enthusiasm, backed by horse sense and persistence, is the quality that most frequently makes for success.

—Dale Carnegie

If I had to select one quality, one personal characteristic that I regard as being most highly correlated with success, whatever the field, I would pick the trait of persistence. Determination. The will to endure to the end, to get knocked down seventy times and get up off the floor saying, "Here comes number seventy-one!"

—Richard M. DeVos

Believe and act as if it were impossible to fail.

—Charles F. Kettering

I know the price of success: dedication, hard work, and a devotion to things you want to see happen.

—Frank Lloyd Wright

The secret of getting ahead is getting started. The secret of getting started is breaking your complex overwhelming tasks into small manageable tasks, and then starting on the first one.

—Mark Twain

Success comes from knowing that you did your best to become the best that you are capable of becoming.

—John Wooden

Many times the difference between failure and success is doing something nearly right . . . or doing it exactly right.

—Source Unknown

The great successful men of the world have used their imaginations, they think ahead and create their mental picture, and then go to work materializing that picture in all its details, filling in here, adding a little there, altering this a bit and that bit, but steadily building, steadily building.

—Robert Collier

Success is dependent upon the glands —sweat glands.

—Zig Ziglar

Leadership

Quote/Unquote

Applewood Books
Bedford, Massachusetts

Thank you for purchasing an Applewood Book. Applewood reprints America's lively classics—books from the past that are still of interest to modern reade For a free copy of our current catalog, please write to Applewood Books, P.O. Box 365, Bedford, MA 0173

ISBN 1-55709-978-2

Library of Congress Control Number: 2001092160

10 9 8 7 6 5 4 3 2 1

Introduction

For any organization to be successful it eeds leadership. People to steer the ship, inspire the 'oops and take responsibility.

/hen creating this compilation we asked ourselves vo questions. The first is, "What qualities and char-:teristics are representative of leadership" and the :cond is, "How does one become a (better) leader?" /e endeavor to answer the first question in the Quote" side of this collection by sharing quotations pout leaders and leadership. In the "Unquote" side this collection, we endeavor to answer the second uestion by providing advice from experts through-it the ages.

/e think that leaders and prospective leaders alike ill benefit from this collection and we encourage you he leaders) to share it with those in your charge. lost of all, we hope that you enjoy this collection and nd the wisdom and motivation to lead your team to ccess!

Quote

A leader is someone who helps improve the lives of other people or improve the system they live under.

—Sam Ervin

Good business leaders create a vision, articulate the vision, passionately own the vision, and relentlessly drive it to completion.

—Jack Welch

Leadership is practiced not so much in words as in attitude and in actions.

—Harold S. Geneen

Leaders are made, they are not born. They are made by hard effort, which is the price which all of us must pay to achieve any goal that is worthwhile.

—Vince Lombardi

The very essence of leadership is [that] you have a vision. It's got to be a vision you articulate clearly and forcefully on every occasion. You can't blow an uncertain trumpet.

—Theodore Hesburgh

Leadership: The art of getting someone else to do something you want done because he wants to do it.

—Dwight D. Eisenhower

Good leaders develop through a never-ending process of self-study, education, training, and experience.

—U.S. Army

A competent leader can get efficient service from poor troops, while on the contrary an incapable leader can demoralize the best of troops.

—John J. Pershing

Whether a man is burdened by power or enjoys power; whether he is trapped by responsibility or made free by it; whether he is moved by other people and outer forces or moves them — this is of the essence of leadership.

—Theodore H. White

Nothing splendid has ever been achieved except by those who dared believe that something inside them was superior to circumstance.

—Bruce Barton

Men make history, and not the other way around. In periods where there is no leadership, society stands still. Progress occurs when courageous, skillful leaders seize the opportunity to change things for the better.

—Harry S Truman

The first task of a leader is to keep hope alive.

—Joe Batten

Leaders know who they are, what their strengths and weaknesses are, and how to fully deploy their strengths and compensate for their weaknesses.

—Warren Bennis

I start with the premise that the function of leadership is to produce more leaders, not more followers.

—Ralph Nader

Leadership is understanding people and involving them to help you do a job. That takes all of the good characteristics, like integrity, dedication of purpose, selflessness, knowledge, skill, implacability, as well as determination not to accept failure.

—Arleigh A. Burke

To be a leader you must preserve all through your life the attitude of being receptive to new ideas. The quality of leadership you will give will depend upon your ability to evaluate new ideas, to separate change for the sake of change from change for the sake of men.

—William A. Hewitt

Effective leadership is the only competitive advantage that will endure. That's because leadership has two sides—what a person is (character) and what a person does (competence).

—Stephen R. Covey

Leadership is getting people to work for you when they are not obligated.

—Fred Smith

In order to be a leader a man must have followers. And to have followers, a man must have their confidence. Hence, the supreme quality for a leader is unquestionably integrity. If a man's associates find him guilty of being phony, if they find that he lacks forthright integrity, he will fail.

—Dwight D. Eisenhower

A good leader takes a little more than their share of the blame and a little less than their share of the credit.

—Source Unknown

Good leadership consists of showing average people how to do the work of superior people.

—John D. Rockefeller

If there is any one secret of success, it lies in the ability to get the other person's point of view and see things from that person's angle as well as from your own.

—Henry Ford

Foresight is the "lead" that the leader has. Once he loses this lead and events start to force his hand, he is leader in name only.

—Robert K. Greenleaf

The best executive is the one who has sense enough to pick good men to do what he wants done, and self-restraint enough to keep from meddling with them while they do it.

—Theodore Roosevelt

Leadership is action, not position.

—Donald H. McGannon

The key to being a good manager is keeping the people who hate me away from those who are still undecided.

—Casey Stengel

The boss drives people; the leader coaches them.
The boss depends on authority; the leader on good will.
The boss inspires fear; the leader inspires enthusiasm.
The boss says "I"; The leader says "WE".
The boss fixes the blame for the breakdown; the leader fixes the breakdown.
The boss says, "GO"; the leader says, "LET'S GO!"

—Harry Gordon Selfridge

There are no office hours for leaders.

—James Cardinal Gibbons

As we look ahead into the next century, leaders will be those who empower others.

—Bill Gates

Leadership is a word and a concept that has been more argued than almost any other I know. I am not one of the desk-pounding types that likes to stick out his jaw and look like he is bossing the show. I would far rather get behind and, recognizing the frailties and the requirements of human nature, would rather try to persuade a man to go along, because once I have persuaded him, he will stick. If I scare him, he will stay just as long as he is scared, and then he is gone.

—Dwight D. Eisenhower

Not the cry, but the flight of the wild duck, leads the flock to fly and follow.

—Proverb

The growth and development of people is the highest calling of leadership.

—Harvey S. Firestone

Managers are people who do things right, and leaders are people who do the right thing.

—Warren Bennis

Effective leadership is not about making speeches or being liked; leadership is defined by results not attributes.

—Peter F. Drucker

The key to successful leadership today is influence, not authority.

—Ken Blanchard

Leaders must wake people out of inertia. They must get people excited about something they've never seen before, something that does not yet exist.

—Rosabeth Moss Kanter

A good leader inspires others with confidence in him; a great leader inspires them with confidence in themselves.

—Source Unknown

Nothing great was ever achieved without enthusiasm.

—Ralph Waldo Emerson

A leader has the vision and conviction that a dream can be achieved. He inspires the power and energy to get it done.

—Ralph Lauren

Great leaders are almost always great simplifiers, who can cut through argument, debate and doubt, to offer a solution everybody can understand.

—Michael Korda

Leadership cannot just go along to get along. Leadership must meet the moral challenge of the day.

—Jesse Jackson

Outstanding leaders go out of their way to boost the self-esteem of their personnel. If people believe in themselves, it's amazing what they can accomplish.

—Sam Walton

Managers help people see themselves as they are; leaders help people to see themselves better than they are.

—Jim Rohn

To lead is to show the way by going in advance; to conduct, escort or direct. To manage is to exert control over; make submissive to one's authority, discipline or persuasion.

—American Heritage Dictionary

A real leader faces the music, even when he doesn't like the tune.

—Source Unknown

Leadership is power to endure an ongoing quest for information or influence... not just actual triumphs like making profits or achieving stated objectives.

—Marsha Sinetar

Asking "who ought to be the boss" is like asking "who ought to be the tenor in the quartet?" Obviously, the man who can sing tenor.

—Henry Ford

A leader knows what's best to do; a manager knows merely how best to do it.

—Ken Adelman

Leadership is getting someone to do what they don't want to do, to achieve what they want to achieve.

—Tom Landry

An overburdened, over-stretched executive is the best executive, because he or she doesn't have the time to meddle, to deal in trivia, to bother people.

—Jack Welch

Leaders must pick causes they won't abandon easily, remain committed despite setbacks, and communicate their big ideas over and over again in every encounter.

—Rosabeth Moss Kanter

One of the key elements of being a good business leader is the capacity to tell the hard truths.

—Jeff Bezos

Ninety percent of leadership is the ability to communicate something people want.

—Dianne Feinstein

The challenge of leadership is to be strong, but not rude; be kind, but not weak; be bold, but not a bully; be thoughtful, but not lazy; be humble, but not timid; be proud, but not arrogant; have humor, but without folly.

—Jim Rohn

We're not altogether sure of when leadership is present, but we are always sure when it is absent.

—Source Unknown

Leadership is the capacity to translate vision into reality.

—Warren Bennis

The final test of a leader is that he leaves behind him in other men the conviction and the will to carry on. The genius of a good leader is to leave behind him a situation which common sense, without the grace of genius, can deal with successfully.

—Walter Lippmann

Leadership has a harder job to do than just choose sides. It must bring sides together.

—Jesse Jackson

Love and respect do not automatically accompany a position of leadership. They must be earned.

—Source Unknown

The difference between a successful person and others is not a lack of strength, not a lack of knowledge, but rather is a lack of will.

—Vince Lombardi

A great leader takes people where they don't necessarily want to go, but ought to be.

—Rosalynn Carter

He who knows not and knows not he knows not: he is a fool—shun him.
He who knows not and knows he knows not: he is simple—teach him.
He who knows and knows not he knows: he is asleep—wake him.
He who knows and knows he knows: he is wise—follow him.

—Proverb

The first responsibility of a leader is to define reality. The last is to say thank you. In between, the leader is a servant.

—Max DePree

True leadership must be for the benefit of the followers, not the enrichment of the leaders.

—Robert Townsend

All of the great leaders have had one characteristic in common: it was the willingness to confront unequivocally the major anxiety of their people in their time. This, and not much else, is the essence of leadership.

—John Kenneth Galbraith

Leaders should be collaborative, modest, and generous.

—Bill Bradley

Good leaders make people feel that they're at the very heart of things, not at the periphery. Everyone feels that he or she makes a difference to the success of the organization. When that happens people feel centered and that gives their work meaning.

—Warren Bennis

Be willing to make decisions. That's the most important quality in a good leader.

—George S. Patton

A leader is a person you will follow to a place you wouldn't go by yourself.

—Joel A. Barker

The motivating team leader is that one person with a dream for the future.

—Dr. Lewis Losoncy

Leadership is much more an art, a belief, a condition of the heart, than a set of things to do. The visible signs of artful leadership are expressed, ultimately, in its practice.

—Max DePree

Leadership is lifting a person's vision to higher sights, the raising of a person's performance to a higher standard, the building of a personality beyond its normal limitations.

—Peter F. Drucker

Unquote

Face reality as it is, not as it was or as you wish it to be.

—Jack Welch

Hard work often leads to success. No work seldom does.

—Harvey Mackay

Leaders, whether in the family, in business, in government, or in education, must not allow themselves to mistake intentions for accomplishments.

—Jim Rohn

Do something—lead, follow, or get out of the way.

—George S. Patton

If you would hit the mark, you must aim a little above it; every arrow that flies feels the attraction of earth.

—Henry Wadsworth Longfellow

Lead and inspire people. Don't try to manage and manipulate people. Inventories can be managed but people must be led.

—H. Ross Perot

An open-door policy doesn't do much for a closed mind.

—Bob Nelson

If you don't like something, change it. If you can't change it, change your attitude.

—Maya Angelou

Whether you think you can or think you can't, you're right.

—Henry Ford

Use power to help people. For we are given power not to advance our own purposes nor to make a great show in the world, nor a name. There is but one just use of power and it is to serve people.

—George Bush

Encourage risk. Nothing demoralizes the troops like knowing that the slightest failure could jeopardize their entire career.

—Kenneth Labich

You can impress people from a distance, but you can only impact them close up.

—Howard Hendricks

You will never stub your toe standing still. The faster you go, the more chance there is of stubbing your toe, but the more chance you have of getting somewhere.

—Charles F. Kettering

You may be disappointed if you fail, but you are doomed if you don't try.

—Beverly Sills

All behavior is a function of its consequences—you get what you reward.

—Bob Nelson

Whatever you do, don't do it halfway.

—Bob Beamon

You may fool all the people some of the time, you can even fool some of the people all of the time, but you cannot fool all of the people all the time.

—Abraham Lincoln

I forgot to shake hands and be friendly. It was an important lesson about leadership.

—Lee Iacocca

A leader, once convinced a particular course of action is the right one, must have the determination to stick with it and be undaunted when the going gets rough.

—Ronald Reagan

Uncertainty will always be part of the taking charge process.

—Harold S. Geneen

Never tell people how to do things. Tell them what to do and they will surprise you with their ingenuity.

—George S. Patton

It is a terrible thing to see and have no vision.

—Helen Keller

The world of the 1990s and beyond will not belong to "managers" or those who can make the numbers dance. The world will belong to passionate, driven leaders—people who not only have enormous amounts of energy but who can energize those whom they lead.

—Jack Welch

Communicate, communicate, and then communicate some more.

—Bob Nelson

Never let what you cannot do interfere with what you can do.

—John Wooden

If you want 1 year of prosperity, grow grain. If you want 10 years of prosperity, grow trees. If you want 100 years of prosperity, grow people.

—Proverb

Nothing so conclusively proves a man's ability to lead others as what he does from day to day to lead himself.

—Thomas J. Watson, Sr.

People respond according to your expectations of them.

—Source Unknown

The world is divided into people who do things, and people who get credit. Try, if you can, to belong to the first class, there is far less competition.

—Dwight Whitney Morrow

A teacher who is attempting to teach, without inspiring the pupil with a desire to learn, is hammering on a cold iron.

—Horace Mann

The truth of the matter is that you always know the right thing to do. The hard part is doing it.

—Norman Schwarzkopf

You'll never get the best from employees by trying to build a fire under them—you've got to build a fire within them.

—Bob Nelson

When building a team, always look for people who love to win. If you can't find any of those, search for people who hate to lose.

—H. Ross Perot

When you get into a tight place and everything goes against you, till it seems as though you could not hold on a minute longer, never give up then, for that is just the place and time that the tide will turn.

—Harriet Beecher Stowe

The time when you need to do something is when no one else is willing to do it, when people are saying it can't be done.

—Mary Frances Berry

If you want to increase your success rate, double your failure rate.

—Tom Watson

Hold yourself responsible to a higher standard than anybody else expects of you; never excuse yourself.

—Henry Ward Beecher

Our chief want in life is somebody who shall make us what we can be.

—Ralph Waldo Emerson

What you say is only the beginning. Your behavior, your actions, and your decisions are also ways of communicating, and leaders have to learn how to create a consistent message through all of these. It's been said many times, but leaders lead by example.

—David Thomas

Do what you feel in your heart to be right. You'll be criticized anyway.

—Eleanor Roosevelt

You cannot push anyone up the ladder unless he is willing to climb.

—Andrew Carnegie

Success without honor is an unseasoned dish; it will satisfy your hunger, but it won't taste good.

—Joe Paterno

One machine can do the work of fifty ordinary men. No machine can do the work of one extraordinary man.

—Elbert Hubbard

There are no shortcuts to any place that is worth going.

—Source Unknown

Pull the string, and it will follow wherever you wish. Push it, and it will go nowhere at all.

—Dwight D. Eisenhower

Well done is better than well said.

—Benjamin Franklin

Perhaps once in a hundred years a person may be ruined by excessive praise, but surely once every minute someone dies inside for lack of it.

—Cecil G. Osborne

Do what you can, with what you have, where you are.

—Theodore Roosevelt

When placed in command—take charge.

—Norman Schwarzkopf

As I grow older, I pay less attention to what men say. I just watch what they do.

—Andrew Carnegie

You've got to stand for something or you will fall for anything.

—Malcolm X

Understanding human needs is half the job of meeting them.

—Adlai E. Stevenson

Be more concerned with your character than with your reputation. Your character is what you really are while your reputation is merely what others think you are.

—John Wooden

Sweat plus sacrifice equals success.

—Charlie Finley

It takes 20 years to build a reputation and five minutes to ruin it. If you think about that, you'll do things differently.

—Warren Buffett

He that cannot obey, cannot command.

—Benjamin Franklin

Setting an example is not the main means of influencing another, it is the only means.

—Albert Einstein

Start with good people, lay out the rules, communicate with your employees, motivate them and reward them. If you do all those things effectively, you can't miss.

—Lee Iacocca

Invite dissent. Your people aren't giving their best . . . if they are afraid to speak up.

—Kenneth Labich

Leadership is a potent combination of strategy and character. But if you must be without one, be without the strategy.

—Norman Schwarzkopf

Surround yourself with the best people you can find, delegate authority, and don't interfere.

—Ronald Reagan

Learn to help people with more than just their jobs: help them with their lives.

—Jim Rohn

To be a leader, you have to make people want to follow you, and nobody wants to follow someone who doesn't know where he is going.

—Joe Namath

No man will make a great leader who wants to do it all himself, or to get all the credit for doing it.

—Andrew Carnegie

Setting a goal is not the main thing. It is deciding how you will go about achieving it and staying with that plan.

—Tom Landry

Take your work seriously and yourself lightly.

—Bob Nelson

One of the best ways to persuade others is with your ears—by listening to them.

—Dean Rusk

You can't build a reputation on what you're going to do.

—Henry Ford

Be candid with everyone.

—Jack Welch

Trust your subordinates. You can't expect them to go all out for you if they think you don't believe in them.

—Kenneth Labich

The secret of getting ahead is getting started. The secret of getting started is breaking your complex overwhelming tasks into small manageable tasks, and then starting on the first one.

—Mark Twain

Build for your team a feeling of oneness, of dependence on one another and of strength to be derived by unity.

—Vince Lombardi

Excellence

Quote/Unquote

Applewood Books
Bedford, Massachusetts

Thank you for purchasing an Applewood Book. Applewood reprints America's lively classics—books from the past that are still of interest to modern reader For a free copy of our current catalog, please write to Applewood Books, P.O. Box 365, Bedford, MA 01730

ISBN 1-55709-976-6

Library of Congress Control Number: 2001092158

10 9 8 7 6 5 4 3 2

Manufactured in U.S.A.

Introduction

Excellence . . . the word itself is a powerful force. It can loosely be described as the pinnacle of success . . . a combination of doing your best and producing great results. You often hear of someone doing a good job or even a great job. Excellence, on the other hand, is very rare.

When creating this compilation we asked ourselves two questions. The first is, "What exactly is excellence?" and the second is, "How does one obtain it?" We endeavor to answer the first question in the "Quote" side of this collection by sharing quotations about the characteristics of excellence. In the "Unquote" side of this collection, we endeavor to answer the second question by providing tips from experts throughout the ages on how to attain excellence.

We think that individuals and organizations alike will benefit from this collection and we encourage you to share the insights that you find in this book. Most of all, we hope that you enjoy this collection and find the wisdom and motivation to live a life of excellence!

Quote

Excellence is to do a common thing in an uncommon way.

—Booker T. Washington

All successful employers are stalking men who will do the unusual, men who think, men who attract attention by performing more than is expected of them.

—Charles M. Schwab

Usually I object when someone makes overmuch of men's work versus women's work, for I think it is the excellence of the results which counts.

—Margaret Bourke-White

The greatest enemy of excellence is good.

—Zig Ziglar

Fast is fine, but accuracy is everything.

—Wyatt Earp

I have never known a concern to make a decided success that did not do good, honest work, and even in these days of fiercest competition, when everything would seem to be a matter of price, there lies still at the root of great business success the very much more important factor of quality. The effect of attention to quality, upon every man in the service, from the president of the concern down to the humblest laborer, cannot be overestimated.

—Andrew Carnegie

Excellence is not being the best, it's doing your best.

—Source Unknown

The person who knows one thing and does it better than anyone else, even if it only be the art of raising lentils, receives the crown he merits. If he raises all his energy to that end, he is a benefactor of mankind and is rewarded as such.

—Og Mandino

Quality means doing it right when no one is looking.

—Henry Ford

I have always tried to go a step past wherever people expected me to end up.

—Beverly Sills

The uncommon man is merely the common man thinking and dreaming of success in larger terms and in more fruitful areas.

—Melvin Powers

The ultimate victory in competition is derived from the inner satisfaction of knowing that you have done your best and that you have gotten the most out of what you had to give.

—Howard Cosell

The idea for which this nation stands will not survive if the highest goal free man can set themselves is an amiable mediocrity. Excellence implies striving for the highest standards in every phase of life.

—John W. Gardner

Excellence encourages one about life generally; it shows the spiritual wealth of the world.

—T. S. Eliot

One machine can do the work of fifty ordinary men. No machine can do the work of one extraordinary man.

—Elbert Hubbard

One can never consent to creep when one feels an impulse to soar.

—Helen Keller

Nothing splendid has ever been achieved except by those who dared believe that something inside them was superior to circumstance.

—Bruce Barton

The difference between a successful person and others is not a lack of strength, not a lack of knowledge, but rather is a lack of will.

—Vince Lombardi

Excellence is the result of caring more than others think is wise; risking more than others think is safe; dreaming more than others think is practical; and expecting more than others think is possible.

—Source Unknown

There is nothing noble in being superior to some other person. The true nobility is in being superior to your previous self.

—Proverb

Once you are labeled "the best" you want to stay up there, and you can't do it by loafing around. If I don't keep changing, I'm history.

—Larry Bird

If man has good corn, or wood, or boards, or pigs to sell, or can make better chairs or knives, crucibles, or church organs, than anybody else, you will find a broad, hard-beaten road to his house, though it be in the woods.

—Ralph Waldo Emerson

Great spirits have always encountered violent opposition from mediocre minds.

—Albert Einstein

Each honest calling, each walk of life, has its own elite, its own aristocracy based on excellence of performance.

—James Bryant Conant

You give your best not because you need to impress people; you give your best because that's the only way to enjoy your work.

—Andrew Matthews

☆

A great man is one who can have power and not abuse it.

—Henry L. Doherty

☆

Lives of great men all remind us we can make our lives sublime. And, departing, leave behind us footprints on the sands of time.

—Henry Wadsworth Longfellow

The master in the art of living makes little distinction between his work and his play, his labor and his leisure, his mind and his body, his information and his recreation, his love and his religion. He hardly knows which is which. He simply pursues his vision of excellence at whatever he does, leaving others to decide whether he is working or playing. To him he's always doing both.

—James A. Michener

I never had a policy; I have just tried to do my very best each and every day.

—Abraham Lincoln

Success is the person who year after year reaches the highest limits in his field.

—Sparky Anderson

I am careful not to confuse excellence with perfection. Excellence, I can reach for; perfection is God's business.

—Michael J. Fox

When a team outgrows individual performance and learns team confidence, excellence becomes a reality.

—Joe Paterno

It is those who have this imperative demand for the best in their natures, and who will accept nothing short of it, that hold the banners of progress, that set the standards, the ideals, for others.

—Orison Swett Marden

Excellence is doing ordinary things extraordinarily well.

—John W. Gardner

One of the great undiscovered joys of life comes from doing everything one attempts to the best of one's ability. There is a special sense of satisfaction, a pride in surveying such a work, a work which is rounded, full, exact, complete in its parts, which the superficial person who leaves his or her work in a slovenly, slipshod, half-finished condition, can never know. It is this conscientious completeness which turns any work into art. The smallest task, well done, becomes a miracle of achievement.

—Og Mandino

Excellence is the gradual result of always striving to do better.

—Pat Riley

In character, in manner, in style, in all things, the supreme excellence is simplicity.

—Henry Wadsworth Longfellow

The man who comes up with a means for doing or producing almost anything better, faster or more economically has his future and his fortune at his fingertips.

—J. Paul Getty

Great champions have an enormous sense of pride. The people who excel are those who are driven to show the world and prove to themselves just how good they are.

—Nancy Lopez

Four short words sum up what has lifted most successful individuals above the crowd: a little bit more. They did all that was expected of them and a little bit more.

—A. Lou Vickery

☆

Excellent firms don't believe in excellence—only in constant improvement and constant change.

—Thomas J. Peters

☆

There is no real excellence in all this world which can be separated from right living.

—David Starr Jordan

If a man is called to be a streetsweeper, he should sweep streets even as Michelangelo painted, or Beethoven composed music, or Shakespeare composed poetry. He should sweep streets so well that all the hosts of heaven and earth will pause to say, "Here lived a great streetsweeper who did his job well."

—Martin Luther King, Jr.

True happiness is the full use of your powers along lines of excellence in a life affording scope.

—John F. Kennedy

The excellent becomes the permanent.

—Jane Addams

Those who consciously purpose themselves in doing nothing less than "exceeding the mark," never have to question whether or not they will "meet the mark"!

—Brian G. Jett

Some people have greatness thrust upon them. Very few have excellence thrust upon them.

—John W. Gardner

Losing a game is heartbreaking. Losing your sense of excellence or worth is a tragedy.

—Joe Paterno

The excellent is new forever.

—Ralph Waldo Emerson

Success is not so much what we have as it is what we are.

—Jim Rohn

After the cheers have died down and the stadium is empty, after the headlines have been written and after you are back in the quiet of your room and the championship ring has been placed on the dresser and all the pomp and fanfare has faded, the enduring things that are left are: the dedication to excellence, the dedication to victory, and the dedication to doing with our lives the very best we can to make the world a better place in which to live.

—Vince Lombardi

Whoever I am, or whatever I am doing, some kind of excellence is within my reach.

—John W. Gardner

I was raised to believe that excellence is the best deterrent to racism and sexism.

—Oprah Winfrey

To be really great in little things, to be truly noble and heroic in the insipid details of everyday life, is a virtue so rare as to be worthy of canonization.

—Harriet Beecher Stowe

It's not that I'm so smart, it's just that I stay with problems longer.

—Albert Einstein

The secret of joy in work is contained in one word—excellence. To know how to do something well is to enjoy it.

—Pearl S. Buck

I've never forgotten for long at a time that living is struggle. I know that every good and excellent thing in the world stands moment by moment on the razor-edge of danger and must be fought for—whether it's a field, or a home, or a country.

—Thornton Wilder

People are like stained-glass windows. They sparkle and shine when the sun is out, but when the darkness sets in, their true beauty is revealed only if there is a light from within.

—Elisabeth Kuebler-Ross

Only those who dare to fail greatly can ever achieve greatly.

—Robert F. Kennedy

Pride is a personal commitment. It is an attitude which separates excellence from mediocrity.

—Source Unknown

Quality begins on the inside . . . and then works its way out.

—Bob Moawad

Perfection, fortunately, is not the only alternative to mediocrity. A more sensible alternative is excellence. Striving for excellence is stimulating and rewarding; striving for perfection—in practically anything—is both neurotic and futile.

—Edwin C. Bliss

The noblest search is the search for excellence.

—Lyndon B. Johnson

The sad truth is that excellence makes people nervous.

—Shana Alexander

It is a grand mistake to think of being great without goodness and I pronounce it as certain that there was never a truly great man that was not at the same time truly virtuous.

—Benjamin Franklin

Excellence is the unlimited ability to improve the quality of what you have to offer.

—Rick Pitino

The society which scorns excellence in plumbing as a humble activity and tolerates shoddiness in philosophy because it is an exalted activity will have neither good plumbing nor good philosophy: neither its pipes nor its theories will hold water.

—John W. Gardner

Happiness does not come from doing easy work but from the afterglow of satisfaction that comes after the achievement of a difficult task that demanded our best.

—Theodore I. Rubin

You don't get in life what you want; you get in life what you are.

—Les Brown

The tourist who moves about to see and hear and open himself to all the influences of the places which condense centuries of human greatness is only a man in search of excellence.

—Max Lerner

There is always a best way of doing everything, even if it be to boil an egg.

—Ralph Waldo Emerson

I made a resolve then that I was going to amount to something if I could. And no hours, no amount of labor, no amount of money would deter me from giving the best that there was in me. And I have done that ever since, and I win by it.

—Colonel Harland Sanders

Unquote

The price of excellence is discipline. The cost of mediocrity is disappointment.

—William A. Ward

The will to win, the desire to succeed, the urge to reach your full potential . . . these are the keys that will unlock the door to personal excellence.

—Eddie Robinson

You must remain focused on your journey to greatness.

—Les Brown

It is easier to do a job right than to explain why you didn't.

—Martin Van Buren

If you don't set a baseline standard for what you'll accept in life, you'll find it's easy to slip into behaviors and attitudes or a quality of life that's far below what you deserve.

—Tony Robbins

The only certain means of success is to render more and better service than is expected of you, no matter what your task may be.

—Og Mandino

Set exorbitant standards, and give your people hell when they don't live up to them. There is nothing so demoralizing as a boss who tolerates second rate work.

—David Ogilvy

Just make up your mind at the very outset that your work is going to stand for quality... that you are going to stamp a superior quality upon everything that goes out of your hands, that whatever you do shall bear the hallmark of excellence.

—Orison Swett Marden

Whether you think you can or think you can't, you're right.

—Henry Ford

Well done is better than well said.

—Benjamin Franklin

Great effort springs naturally from great attitude.

—Pat Riley

The most rewarding things you do in life are often the ones that look like they cannot be done.

—Arnold Palmer

Shoot for the moon, even if you miss, you'll land amongst the stars.

—Les Brown

There are no short cuts to any place worth going.

—Beverly Sills

Most great people have attained their greatest success just one step beyond their greatest failure.

—Napoleon Hill

There is no great achievement that is not the result of patient working and waiting.

—Josiah Gilbert Holland

If you want to achieve excellence, you can get there today. As of this second, quit doing less-than-excellent work.

—Thomas J. Watson, Sr.

The minute you start talking about what you're going to do if you lose, you have lost.

—George Shultz

You have to learn the rules of the game. And then you have to play better than anyone else.

—Dianne Feinstein

Always do more than is required of you.

—George S. Patton

Let others lead small lives, but not you. Let others argue over small things, but not you. Let others cry over small hurts, but not you. Let others leave their future in someone else's hands, but not you.

—Jim Rohn

All greatness is achieved while performing outside your comfort zone.

—Greg Arnold

Do not pray for easy lives. Pray to be stronger men. Do not pray for tasks equal to your powers. Pray for powers equal to your tasks.

—Phillips Brooks

Nothing great was ever achieved without enthusiasm.

—Ralph Waldo Emerson

If you want to increase your success rate, double your failure rate.

—Tom Watson

You must do the thing you think you cannot do.

—Eleanor Roosevelt

If one advances confidently in the direction of his dreams, and endeavors to live the life he has imagined, he will meet with a success unexpected in common hours.

—Henry David Thoreau

Good enough never is.

—Debbi Field

A common pitfall on the path of excellence is an overemphasis on comparing our progress with others.

—Michael Gelb

Much good work is lost for the lack of a little more.

—Edward H. Harriman

I find that the great thing in this world is not so much where we stand as in what direction we are moving. To reach the port of heaven, we must sail sometimes with the wind and sometimes against it—but we must sail, and not drift, nor lie at anchor.

—Oliver Wendell Holmes

It takes as much energy to wish as it does to plan.

—Eleanor Roosevelt

Do a little more each day than you think you possibly can.

—Lowell Thomas

There are powers inside of you which, if you could discover and use, would make of you everything you ever dreamed or imagined you could become.

—Orison Swett Marden

Destiny is not a matter of chance, it is a matter of choice; it is not a thing to be waited for, it is a thing to be achieved.

—William Jennings Bryant

Whenever you do a thing, act as if all the world were watching.

—Thomas Jefferson

You can become an even more excellent person by constantly setting higher and higher standards for yourself and then by doing everything possible to live up to those standards.

—Brian Tracy

People respond according to your expectations of them.

—Source Unknown

If there is a way to do it better . . . find it.

—Thomas A. Edison

Optimism is the faith that leads to achievement. Nothing can be done without hope and confidence.

—Helen Keller

Desire is the key to motivation, but it's the determination and commitment to an unrelenting pursuit of your goal—a commitment to excellence—that will enable you to attain the success you seek.

—Mario Andretti

Coming together is a beginning. Keeping together is progress. Working together is success.

—Henry Ford

If you can't do great things, do small things in a great way. Don't wait for great opportunities. Seize common, everyday ones and make them great.

—Napoleon Hill

There is no such thing as a natural touch. Touch is something you create by hitting millions of golf balls.

—Lee Trevino

Don't measure yourself by what you have accomplished, but by what you should have accomplished with your ability.

—John Wooden

If you would hit the mark, you must aim a little above it; every arrow that flies feels the attraction of earth.

—Henry Wadsworth Longfellow

Whatever you do, don't do it halfway.

—Bob Beamon

Think of yourself as on the threshold of unparalleled success. A whole, clear, glorious life lies before you. Achieve! Achieve!

—Andrew Carnegie

If any man seeks for greatness, let him forget greatness and ask for truth, and he will find both.

—Horace Mann

You are not here to fritter away your precious hours when you have the ability to accomplish so much by making a slight change in your routine. No more hiding from success. Leave time, leave space, to grow. Now.

—Og Mandino

Hold yourself responsible to a higher standard than anybody else expects of you; never excuse yourself.

—Henry Ward Beecher

The three great essentials to achieve anything worth while are, first, hard work; second, stick-to-itiveness; third, common sense.

—Thomas A. Edison

If you do what you've always done, you'll get what you've always gotten.

—Tony Robbins

A man can succeed at almost anything for which he has unlimited enthusiasm.

—Charles M. Schwab

Setting a goal is not the main thing. It is deciding how you will go about achieving it and staying with that plan.

—Tom Landry

If you'll not settle for anything less than your best, you will be amazed at what you can accomplish in your lives.

—Vince Lombardi

When you get into a tight place and everything goes against you, till it seems as though you could not hold on a minute longer, never give up then, for that is just the place and time that the tide will turn.

—Harriet Beecher Stowe

You get the best out of others when you get the best out of yourself.

—Harvey S. Firestone

Everything comes to him who hustles while he waits.

—Henry Ford

If you want to be creative in your company, your career, your life, all it takes is one easy step... the extra one. When you encounter a familiar plan, you just ask one question: What ELSE could we do?

—Dale Dauten

Believe and act as if it were impossible to fail.

—Charles F. Kettering

Act so as to elicit the best in others and thereby in thyself.

—Felix Adler

You've got to get up every morning with determination if you're going to go to bed with satisfaction.

—George Lorimer

Deliver more than you are getting paid to do. The victory of success will be half won when you learn the secret of putting out more than is expected in all that you do. Make yourself so valuable in your work that eventually you will become indispensable.

—Og Mandino

Find something that you're really interested in doing in your life. Pursue it, set goals, and commit yourself to excellence. Do the best you can.

—Chris Evert

Hard work often leads to success. No work seldom does.

—Harvey Mackay

The big challenge is to become all that you have the possibility of becoming. You cannot believe what it does to the human spirit to maximize your human potential and stretch yourself to the limit.

—Jim Rohn

Do what you can, with what you have, where you are.

—Theodore Roosevelt

Show class, have pride, and display character. If you do, winning takes care of itself.

—Paul Bryant

You are a product of your environment. So choose the environment that will best develop you toward your objective. Analyze your life in terms of its environment. Are the things around you helping you toward success—or are they holding you back.

—W. Clement Stone

☆

Don't try to become great; be great now, and discover that excellence is a reward you don't need others to confirm.

—Guy Finley

☆

Go as far as you can see, and when you get there, you will see farther.

—Source Unknown

Introduction

The illness is serious. Possibly terminal. That's the diagnosis that has been given to a friend . . . a member of your family . . . or you. How do you cope? Where do you turn for comfort in this, your most trying hour?

Paul Johnson, a physician, faced this very situation. Unexpected, unwanted, cancer suddenly slammed into his life. In need of support, he turned to the Great Physician for strength, for hope, for comfort.

Out of his experience has come this booklet. It is a series of brief reflections, each candidly revealing his inmost thoughts and fears as the treatment of his cancer progresses.

But more than just a chronicle of his disease, this booklet is a testimony to the fact that God is there. He cares. And He comforts. Paul Johnson shares that comfort.

Are you—or someone you love—facing a life-threatening illness? Here are understanding words from one who knows what that dark valley is like. He has walked its length and discovered, in the process, that he was never alone.

Come let his Companion be yours.

The LORD is my shepherd, I shall lack nothing.
He makes me lie down in green pastures,
he leads me beside quiet waters,
he restores my soul.

Even though I walk
through the valley of the shadow of death,
I will fear no evil,
for you are with me;
your rod and your staff,
they comfort me.

Psalm 23:1-3a, 4

Comfort

As a doctor I've told many people of illnesses that threatened their lives. I often wondered how I would react if I were the patient and not the doctor. And then it happened. The diagnosis: cancer of the colon. The prognosis: very doubtful. The future: uncertain.

Life had led me, as it has you, into the valley of the shadow of death.

But I wasn't alone in the valley. No matter how great the uncertainty and the pain, I was never deserted. Let me walk with you in your valley. Let me share with you the comfort, the hope, that God has there for you and for me.

Telling My Wife

Going into the examination, I fully expected to be given a clean bill of health. To find something of this magnitude is devastating. I feel a myriad of swirling emotions.

First of all I have to tell Genevieve. I try to get my thoughts together as I dress. On the drive home—some nine or ten miles—I can think of no way to break the news. At this point I feel as lonely as at any other time during my illness.

Genevieve hears my car. When I come home this time of day, without phoning, she knows it's bad news. She asks me what it means. I still feel very lonely and isolated. We embrace, and cry a little.

The tumor is of such size and magnitude I feel quite helpless and uncertain. I know this disease. I know there's a really rough road ahead. I know the outcome is most likely to be death.

Help Me

As a surgeon I am perplexed many times and feel the need to call in a consultant. I see terminal illness, or any illness categorized as untreatable, in this same light.

There's no human physician who can provide a solution. How good to know we can call in the Great Physician, Jesus Himself, for consultation. He knows us so intimately that He has numbered the very hairs of our heads.

I find myself going to Him more and more. He may not respond the way I expect or might like. It's impossible for me to know ahead of time what He has for me. After all, I am time and earth-bound in my outlook.

But I know He has the power, and the wisdom, and the love. I can trust myself into His hands.

When I said, "My foot is slipping,"
your love, O LORD, supported me.
When anxiety was great within me,
your consolation brought joy to my soul.
Psalm 94:18, 19

Shock

Even for a doctor, it's like being thrown into a strange world of cold, impersonal, scientific people. The sounds are disturbing. The hum of the X-ray. The rattle of test tubes. The look of multiplied vials and syringes. The sterile white coats.

Nurses treat me as a thing rather than a person. I want people to care, and they don't seem to. I know they can't become emotionally involved with everyone. But still, couldn't they have a little more compassion?

At first there's even guilt. The feeling of imposing on others. And embarrassment. Then, as the shock wears off, we begin to see the people around us a little more realistically. We accept the routine, and see the reason for actions that before seemed cold and impersonal. Through it all there are one or two who give us special attention and affection. To these we're most thankful. It's strange. The more we get into the routine of medical services, the more we find people becoming compassionate. Are they really more compassionate? Or am I becoming less sensitive?

O Sovereign LORD,
  deal well with me for your name's sake;
  out of the goodness of your love,
  deliver me.
For I am poor and needy,
  and my heart is wounded within me.

Psalm 109:21, 22

Fear

At first I feel resentment. My normal life is disrupted. I can see myself getting behind. In my practice. Financially. In everything. But more important is the overwhelming uncertainty. Am I going to get well at all? The thoughts and feelings tug at me. It's a nightmare that doesn't go away.

I search for answers. I peer, hoping to interpret the expressions of the nurses who read my chart. I'm uneasy at the discussions in the hallway. I look for anything to give me a clue: for any encouragement or hope.

Many times we overreact. We misinterpret an expression or a word. After all, the world we find ourselves in is confusing. Terrifying. Yet it's so important to us. Our very future seems to hinge on the doctor's pronouncement of what is to be.

But the doctor doesn't know. As a doctor myself, I have never told anyone, "You are going to die." I can never be that sure. No one can. I've seen too many "hopeless" cases restored to health. We doctors are not God. My future is in wiser, more loving Hands.

One thing God has spoken,
two things have I heard:
that you, O God, are strong,
and that you, O Lord, are loving.

Psalm 62:11, 12

I'm Tired

I feel devastated and emotionally shaken. I've had five days of tests. Five days of liquid diets and laxative purges. Five days of brisk, impersonal technicians. I'm weak physically, and the hospital seems so foreign. So sterile. It's as though I'm in enemy territory.

By the time I go to surgery I'm almost a zombie from the preparation. I think this is something medical people forget sometimes. I'm weak, and in this place I have no sense of control.

It's hard for us to realize, under the strain of the first pressures, that we'll ever feel better. But we will. If there is pain, it will come much later. And then drugs will relieve our suffering. And there is always the chance the surgery will be successful.

The first days of shock and exhaustion will pass. There are better days ahead.

Some wandered in desert wastelands,
  finding no way to a city where
  they could settle.
They were hungry and thirsty,
  and their lives ebbed away.
Then they cried out to the LORD in their trouble,
  and he delivered them from their distress.
He led them by a straight way
  to a city where they could settle.
Let them give thanks to the LORD for
  his unfailing love
  and his wonderful deeds for men,
for he satisfies the thirsty
  and fills the hungry with good things.

Psalm 107:4-9

Envy

Many times I've seen people angry at their disease and at the fact they have to go through this sort of thing. But what I feel is envy.

I look at people who are perfectly normal, and wonder how it feels. What if I didn't have my life threatening problem?

It's hard to accept the fact that I'm in as serious a situation as I am. I have no pain. No symptoms. And yet the evidence is there, loud and clear on the X-ray films and on the operating room table.

Each of us with a serious illness has negative feelings at times. Anger. Envy. Bitterness. We needn't condemn ourselves, though. We're all only human. I take great comfort in the fact that God understands my feelings, and that He loves me anyway.

I know that my feelings of envy will pass. God will give me the grace to overcome them, and He will give me His own peace.

In Jesus we do not have a high priest who is unable to sympathize with our weaknesses, but we have one who has been tempted in every way, just as we are—yet was without sin. Let us then approach the throne of grace with confidence, so that we may receive mercy and find grace to help us in our time of need.

Hebrews 4:15-16

I'm Worried

Finally I realize that I really have cancer. I wake up in the morning and it hasn't gone away. It's like a bad dream. I'd like to call the whole thing off and go back to work. But I can't. I'm trapped in a situation that I must go through.

A lot of things occur to me. The mortgage on my house suddenly seems much too large. I wish I'd prepared for this, and I didn't. I wish I'd taken the family trip last summer. I wish I had more life insurance. I wish I'd taken more care, and made better provision for my family. But it's too late.

Even when our past is gone and our future is in doubt, there's one reality that can quiet and relieve. Even if I leave my loved ones, God will be with them. He is a loving Father, and He will give them a Father's care.

Jesus said, "Therefore I tell you, do not worry about your life, what you will eat or drink; or about your body, what you will wear. Is not life more important than food, and the body more important than clothes? Look at the birds of the air; they do not sow or reap or store away in barns, and yet your heavenly Father feeds them. Are you not much more valuable than they?

"For the pagans run after all these things, and your heavenly Father knows that you need them. But seek first his kingdom and his righteousness, and all these things will be given to you as well."

Matthew 6:25-26, 32-33

Relaxing

Little by little I've settled down. I've learned to roll a bit better with the punches.

I began to feel better shortly after the operation. I wanted to get back to normal as quickly as I could. I got out of bed. I even pushed myself a bit beyond my capacity.

Now I'm going to the office. Not to see patients. Just to be there. To be around my friends and my normal way of living. I'm anxious to be as much into the stream as I can.

Many people have told me that when they get sick they feel guilty and ashamed. They wonder how they're going to be of any value. It helps us to return to favorite surroundings. Putting on our own clothes, eating our familiar cooking, going to favorite places, all make us feel that we're getting well.

I'm glad I stretched myself to come home. Life isn't over yet. And I've reached my first goal on what I hope is the road to recovery.

Little Irritations

It's as though all my priorities have changed. I don't care if the inflation rate is fifteen percent. I couldn't care less who's running for President, or what the price of gold is. I find myself resenting people who are normal and can enjoy that kind of thing. Small talk bothers me. I want people to be more serious. Here I'm in bad straits, and everyone else chatters on. Don't they know in a short time I might not be here?

At first those of us with a life-threatening illness are likely to have such feelings. We may feel a flash of anger at people we love. We feel they should be more concerned. That their life shouldn't seem to go on so normally, when our own life has been so changed.

Later I know I'll be thankful for the small talk. I realize it wouldn't be good for me to withdraw. Life goes on, and I'm still here in the land of the living. Why should I isolate myself, as if I were already dead? I'm not dead, I'm living.

Nights

Nights are the hardest for me. I'm not able to sleep sometimes, and then in the quiet darkness I imagine all sorts of things.

I think about the children I may leave, and I worry about my wife, whom I love very much. I wonder how it will be in this beautiful home I have with her, if she would have to live alone. I think of all the bad things that can happen in a home with no man around.

It's strange how so many negative thoughts can flood our minds at night when we're threatened with serious illness. It's then especially that we need someone or something to turn to.

My spiritual life is a great source of strength. It's the only thing that neutralizes the dark thoughts. There are beautiful verses from the Scriptures. And brothers and sisters in Christ who love me.

Where can I go from your Spirit?
  Where can I flee from your presence?
If I go up to the heavens, you are there;
  if I make my bed in the depths, you are there.
If I rise on the wings of the dawn,
  if I settle on the far side of the sea,
even there your hand will guide me,
  your right hand will hold me fast.

If I say, "Surely the darkness will hide me
  and the light become night around me,"
even the darkness will not be dark to you;
  the night will shine like the day,
  for darkness is as light to you.

Psalm 139:7-12

Chemotherapy

I've recovered from the operation. But now I have to go into therapy.

Chemotherapy does strange things to me. I've begun having various types of dreams. Crazy thoughts enter my mind, and I have no control over them. And with it all there is vomiting and nausea. I feel so ill at ease.

My normal course of life is interrupted again each time I take a course of therapy. And I do this one week out of three. It's a price I'm not sure I want to pay. If this is the way it's going to be, perhaps I should give up and let the disease take its course.

There are times when we all want to give up. But there *is* hope. And hope is something we need not surrender.

Now faith is being sure of what we hope for and certain of what we do not see.

Hebrews 11:1

Doubts

I have a real, personal relationship with Jesus Christ. Even so, I'm having periods of doubt. Times when I wonder if I've just been given a bill of goods, or sold "pie in the sky."

It helps me to remember all the people in Scripture who had genuine doubts. Yet God accepted them, and cherished them. David. Peter. Paul. Yes, there were many who were close to God and who had doubts.

It's only natural for us to wonder, and to have doubts about the way things are going. That doesn't have anything to do with our relationship with God, or our reliance on God for strength and support. Our faith doesn't rest on our feelings.

I've chosen to rest my confidence in what Jesus has done for me on Calvary, and not in what I can do for Him. That relationship doesn't even rest on how "strong" my faith is when the doubts crowd in.

If we died with him,
  we will also live with him,
if we endure,
  we will also reign with him.

if we are faithless,
  he will remain faithful,
  for he cannot disown himself.

2 Timothy 2:11-13

Alone

It's time for my radiation therapy. Each day at this time I'm ushered into this little room.

The room is small; probably twenty by twenty. I lie here on a table under the giant X-ray machine. After I'm positioned on the table, everyone leaves the room. The heavy, lead-lined door closes. I'm here, alone, with no contact with those outside.

Then the little door covering the cobalt opens. In the silence, unable to move, I realize that my body is being bombarded by lethal doses of radiation. Yet, without them I won't be able to survive.

In the treatment of most life-threatening diseases, we are constantly bombarded by unpleasantness. With things that distress us. Without the Lord, without knowing He's here, I wonder how I could have gone through all this? I wonder how those without His support can make it, and keep their dignity and their sanity?

God has said,
"Never will I leave you;
never will I forsake you."
So we say, with confidence,
"The Lord is my helper;
I will not be afraid.
What can man do to me?"

Hebrews 13:5-6

Cut Off

My white blood count has fallen below 1,000. This means I'm in danger of picking up an infection. So my doctor has isolated me.

I'm cut off from all people and from anything that might bring bacteria into contact with me. All this makes me feel that I'm different. That I'm out of step as far as the world around me is concerned. It's a price I'm not sure I want to pay.

We all may face periods of depression in the course of our treatment. Depression isn't pleasant, but we need not be ashamed.

Isolated now, I need someone bigger even than my relatives and friends. Someone I can turn to, who can be with me always. I only know One Person who can do that.

Faith

In my practice I've seen many people with life-threatening illnesses hear about Jesus for the first time. I don't understand why some groups try to care for the terminally ill, to make them comfortable and meet some of their needs, but ignore the spiritual. Their help doesn't give the person who is in danger inner peace and comfort. And I've found that to be the most important by far.

For many years I've brought in the spiritual. During my relationship with a patient who is seriously ill I've attempted to lead him to have confidence in Jesus Christ. Because I totally believe in Him myself.

Now that my own life is threatened, I know faith makes a difference. I've known fear, and depression, and helplessness, and loneliness. But in it all I've had hope. I've seen my apprehensions relieved as Jesus has supported me. He is the only one who has won victory over death. He is living. He knows my problems, and He cares about me.

Who Can I Turn To?

There comes a point when modern medicine has to admit it is totally impotent. What do I do then? Do I give up? Do I make myself comfortable and wait to die? Or is there something else I can do?

I think more and more physicians are recognizing the fact that spiritual strength at such times is essential. I know I want my patients to have the opportunity to accept or reject the only treatment left beyond the human realm.

There have been times when I am depressed, and times I am deeply anxious. But then I remember who Jesus is, and what He came to do for me. I realize that as much as I want to live, physical life isn't the basic issue. But I would never be able to face the future with confidence if I hadn't come to know Jesus Christ.

I tell my patients, "Don't feel guilty or ashamed to have waited till now, when you're hurting, to come to Jesus. He isn't insulted or upset that you've put Him off. He loves you too much to want you to miss out. He's there now, loving, waiting, holding out His arms to you."

What, then, shall we say in response to this? If God is for us, who can be against us? He who did not spare his own Son, but gave him up for us all—how will he not also, along with him, graciously give us all things? Who will bring any charge against those whom God has chosen? It is God who justifies. Who is he that condemns? Christ Jesus, who died—more than that, who was raised to life—is at the right hand of God and is also interceding for us.

Who shall separate us from the love of Christ? Shall trouble or hardship or persecution or famine or nakedness or danger or sword? No, in all these things we are more than conquerors through him who loved us. For I am convinced that neither death nor life, neither angels nor demons, neither the present nor the future, nor any powers, neither height nor depth, nor anything else in all creation, will be able to separate us from the love of God that is in Christ Jesus our Lord.

Romans 8:31-35, 37-39

Beauty

I'm home again on beautiful Lake Washington. And I've just realized that I'm seeing things I never noticed before.

I see a dozen different kinds of ducks, swimming off my dock. It's funny. I never noticed they were different before.

I notice the flowers. And the cloud formations. I see so many things I never took time for.

Even a life-threatening illness isn't all black. God has little gifts for us that lighten the burden.

Many, O LORD my God,
  are the wonders you have done.
The things you planned for us
  no one can recount to you;
were I to speak and tell of them,
  they would be too many to declare.

Psalm 40:5

Springtime

My illness came in the late winter. Now, in the early spring, it's comforting to me to see something I've cherished since childhood.

It's the little flower called trillium. As a boy growing up in western Washington, I used to look for it, to find and touch it in the woods. I've planted some in my yard, and now I see it sprouting, and budding, and blooming.

I've always been fond of trillium. It blooms around Easter, and reminds me now of new life, of rebirth, and of resurrection.

Now I look at my trillium and reflect on the resurrection of Jesus, and on my own resurrection. I see some patients come to the place where they give up. The trillium reminds me I never need to give up. I will escape my illness. In Jesus I will escape my very mortality.

Christ has indeed been raised from the dead, the firstfruits of those who have fallen asleep. For since death came through a man, the resurrection of the dead comes also through a man. For as in Adam all die, so in Christ all will be made alive. But each in his own turn: Christ, the firstfruits; then, when he comes, those who belong to him.

For he must reign until he has put all his enemies under his feet. The last enemy to be destroyed is death.

1 Corinthians 15:20-23, 25-26

Comforted

No one looks forward to suffering. And no one looks forward to death. It's hard not to be discouraged sometimes, and depressed. But I don't feel guilty. I wouldn't be human if I didn't feel discouraged at times.

I know that God understands and that He is deeply concerned when we're ill and discouraged. We never need to be alone, though. We can talk with Him without an appointment. And He makes Himself real.

At one time I felt terribly discouraged. I suddenly saw myself being picked up in Jesus' arms, and cradled like a small child. He rocked me back and forth and comforted me. I was crying. He wiped away my tears.

I can't understand why so many deny or belittle Him when they don't have any better answer. Life and death are mysteries. But I have never heard of anything with the believability and the comfort of the message of Jesus Christ.

This is how God showed his love among us: He sent his one and only Son into the world that we might live through him. This is love: not that we loved God, but that he loved us and sent his Son as an atoning sacrifice for our sins.

And we have seen and testify that the Father has sent his Son to be the Savior of the world. If anyone acknowledges that Jesus is the Son of God, God lives in him and he in God. And so we know and rely on the love God has for us.

1 John 4:9-10, 14-16

Hope

My cancer surgery and therapy are now three years past. So there was hope for me after all.

And there is hope for you. Always.

But your hope and mine need to be fixed on something more important than our recovery. Our life on earth must end, whatever the outcome of this present illness. Then each of us must face the question of eternity.

My deep desire is that you approach eternity with a sure hope. A hope that's founded on your confidence in Jesus Christ, who loves you, who died for you, and who was raised again. In Jesus you will find forgiveness of sins, and eternal life.

In Jesus, the greatest hope of all will be fulfilled.

For a more complete discussion of this subject, see *Death and the Caring Community* by Larry Richards and Paul Johnson, published by Multnomah Press.